When Software Superslug hears Mrs Potter compare him to Pythagoras, his superbrain goes into overdrive. Who or what is Pythagoras?

Could he be a magnificent prehistoric snail – a sort of Pythagosaurus Rex – and possibly Software's own ancestor? And what about the amazing mystery snail Cat-Flap has seen which makes her fall heads over tails in love?

While Slipper-Sock worries about Cat-Flap's new passion, Tom Potter worries about his dad's – for nutty novelty knitting. When the two different obsessions cross paths, the result is a terrible tangle!

Software Superslug
and the
Nutty Novelty Knitting

Joyce Dunbar

Illustrated by James Dunbar

SIMON & SCHUSTER

LONDON • SYDNEY • NEW YORK • TOKYO • TORONTO

Text copyright © 1990 Joyce Dunbar
Illustrations copyright © 1990 James Dunbar

First published in Great Britain in 1990
by Simon & Schuster Young Books

Set in 13pt Baskerville by ![Tek Art logo] Tek Art Ltd, Croydon, Surrey
Printed and bound in Great Britain by
The Guernsey Press Co. Ltd, Guernsey, Channel Islands

Simon & Schuster Young Books
Simon & Schuster International Group
Wolsey House
Wolsey Road
Hemel Hempstead HP2 4SS

BRITISH LIBRARY CATALOGUING IN PUBLICATION DATA
Dunbar, Joyce
    Software superslug and the nutty novelty knitting
    I. Title II. Dunbar, James
    823′.914 [J]

ISBN 0 7500 0028 7
ISBN 0 7500 0034 1 Pbk

Contents

Chapter 1

Knit, Purl

"Knit. Purl. Knit. Purl. Knit. Purl. Knit two together. Pull wool forward. Slip one."

The sound came from behind the sitting-room door, like a strange chant in a foreign language.

Tom Potter winced with embarrassment. He had just come in with a friend. He started to whistle loudly while taking off his jacket. But he couldn't whistle loudly enough.

"What's that noise?" asked Max.

"Nothing. Oh nothing," said Tom, with an exaggerated shuffle of his feet. "Come on, we've got things to do."

Tom and Max were getting together to work

something out for their stall at the school fête. Tom already had an idea up his sleeve – for a tin-can shy – and was eager to get going.

"But I can hear this funny noise," insisted Max.

"Must be the radio," said Tom, tugging at his friend's arm.

"No it's not," said Max. "It sounds like . . ."

"Knit. Purl. Knit. Purl. Oh doldrums! Oh dipsticks! How on earth am I supposed to cast off?"

"YOUR DAD!" cried Max in disbelief.

There was no mistaking the voice. Max was in Tom's class at school, where Tom Potter's dad was a teacher. Nobody said "doldrums" quite like him. Nobody else said "dipsticks".

"He's not . . . he can't be . . ." said Max, with a grin spreading over his face.

"No he is *not!*" said Tom Potter decisively. "Come on, let's get on with the job."

"He *is!*" said Max, nearly exploding with mirth. "Your dad is actually knitting!"

Tom Potter slammed the sitting-room door.

"Just wait till I tell them at school!" said Max.

"If you tell anyone at school any such thing –" threatened Tom, "then I'll – I'll –"

"Knit me a pom-pom hat!" hooted Max.

"Look here," said Tom, spiky with indignation, "are you going to help me or not?"

"Keep your hair on," said Max, trying to calm things down. But he couldn't resist the remark, "If you can't, your dad will knit you a new lot."

This was too much for Tom. He took a swipe at Max who went scooting off down the hall, bumping into Betsy on the way.

Betsy was Tom Potter's sister. She knew how to stick up for herself. Betsy threw a cushion and knocked over a potted plant, which brought Mrs Potter rushing on to the scene.

"He started it –"

"It's his fault –"

"She knocked it over –" the three children shouted at once, so that Mrs Potter had to shout even louder to make them shut up.

"Your father will be after you next –" she began, but she didn't need to say more. Mr Potter strode into the room. Far from looking angry, his face was shining with proud delight.

"Look!" he exclaimed. "It's finished!"

All four of them looked. Mr Potter held something in his hands. He offered it up for admiration. It was woolly, lime green and knitted.

"What *is* it Dad?" asked Betsy.

"Can't you see?" said Mr Potter, puffing it out and poking it into shape with his fingers.

Betsy shook her head. Mrs Potter blinked. Tom groaned and clapped his hands over his eyes.

"It's a plant-pot holder!" announced Mr Potter.

Max really had no choice. Max simply could not help it. He snorted and creased up with laughter.

Chapter 2

Pythagosaurus Rex

From the underside of the armchair in the sitting room where Mr Potter had been knitting, there came a very deep sigh. A sigh so deep it was profound.

It came from Software Superslug.

Software didn't live there of course. He lived in a lovely warm damp muggy hole next to the cellar of the house, with a large colony of snails. But he sometimes found it cramped and claustrophobic. Whenever he needed to concentrate he would make his way to the underside of his favourite armchair, and he needed to concentrate now.

Pythagoras? Who, or what, was Pythagoras? The question had been on his mind ever since Mrs Potter had taken him to school, and holding him aloft had declared, "He's Pythagoras compared to the others."

Now why? And why had she looked so abashed when he had made a slime trail that was squiggly, not straight?

Software had no trouble at all in pronouncing the name Pythagoras. He had no trouble at all in remembering it. No doubt either – if he was asked – he could even spell it.

Software, you see, was a genius. He was the highest and the lowest form of life – a brain inside the body of a slug. It was a truly brilliant brain. As with all geniuses, his curiosity was easily aroused. He couldn't let a question pass unnoticed. He couldn't bear to find gaps in his knowledge. They simply had to be filled.

But for wanting to know about Pythagoras, Software had a very special reason. He knew he was no common sort of slug; he thought he was a snail without a shell. He *passionately* wanted a shell. But Mrs Potter had compared him to Pythagoras. Perhaps he was one of these instead.

Pythagoras, no doubt, was a prehistoric snail, with a wonderful prehistoric shell.

Pythagosaurus Rex!

Somewhere, along the centuries, he had taken leave of his shell, but soon he would get it back. Software had been conjuring up visions of just such a creature, with himself as its only descendant, when Mr Potter had begun.

"Knit. Purl. Knit. Purl. Knit. Purl . . ." to the clicketty-clack of steel needles.

Now Software understood human talk. He knew words like "serendipity". His best words were picked up from Tom Potter, who was crazy about his computer: Floppy-Disc, User-Friendly, Fast-Forward and the like. He gave these as names to the snails. That was why they allowed him to live with them. Also, because he gave them the low-down; told them food-wise what was where. Not a lettuce could sprout, not a bean could shoot, not a strawberry ripen in secret; Software was always in the know.

But for the moment, Software was puzzled. He didn't understand "knit" or "purl". Nor could he understand the lime-green strand of wool that was snaking up from the floor towards Mr Potter's hand, jerking busily all the time.

"Perhaps," he thought hopefully, "this will give me a clue to Pythagoras." But before he could investigate further, Mr Potter broke off the wool, stood up, and abruptly left the room.

15

Hence the profoundly deep sigh.

Software crawled from beneath the armchair, missing the large, lime-green ball of wool, now stuck with a pair of knitting needles, that Mr Potter had left behind him. He continued across the sitting-room floor, through a crack in the floorboards, along the ceiling of the cellar, through the entrance of the air vent, until he reached "Hole Sweet Hole".

He expected to find the snails sleeping. That was how they usually spent their days, venturing out at nights into the garden, mostly on the look-out for food. But the snails were not sleeping now. Now there was a great to-do.

Cat-Flap was in a swoon.

It wasn't the sort of swoon that knocks you out flat, but the sort that sends you all moony-eyed.

"What's the matter with Cat-Flap?" asked Software.

"Idunno," said a snail called Idunno, who never said anything else.

Cat-Flap was a fat round grandma snail who was rather soft-hearted. Slipper-Sock was the grandpa. Slipper-Sock looked very worried.

"Fan her! Give her some air! Slap a wet leaf on her head!"

But the more the snails fussed, the more Cat-Flap lolled about, her eyes rolling, her shell teetering, her tentacles completely out of kilter.

"Come on Cat-Flap," coaxed Software. "Tell us what it is."

There was a pause, while Cat-Flap struggled for words. She gulped, blinked, smiled, for a moment recovered her poise, then at last it came out.

"I'm in love," she sighed. "I've fallen heads over tails in love!"

Chapter 3

Hi-Fi

There was a shocked silence from the circle of snails. Cat-Flap – at her age – in love!

"With me, I hope," said Slipper-Sock at last.

"With you!?" said Cat-Flap scornfully. "With a sloppy old snail like you! Not likely! Oh no. I'm in love with a – a –"

She was so filled up with feelings, she could hardly get out the words, but from what the snails could gather, Cat-Flap had gone looking for Software in the sitting room, and seen there the most extraordinary snail.

Everything about him was extraordinary: his size – enormous; his shell – delicately grooved; his colour – lime green; his tentacles – sharp and shiny; his tail – well – his tail was elegantly two-pronged.

"He sounds like a bad dream to me," said User-Friendly. "Did you eat too much delphinium last night? You know it disagrees with you."

"Or a snail from outer space," said Floppy-Disc, getting all excited. "Did he land in a flying saucer?"

Software had ideas of his own. Could it be –? Was it possibly –? It sounded just like Pythagosaurus Rex!

"*Where* exactly did you see him?" he asked, trying not to sound too eager.

Cat-Flap mooned and swooned, unable to say a sensible word.

"Cat-Flap! Don't be ridiculous! You're a grandma! You should be past that sort of thing!" scolded Whizz-Kid.

The insult brought Cat-Flap to her senses. "Past it!" she protested. "You cheeky young whipper-snapper! I'll show you who's past it! I'll show you –"

"Just show us this amazing snail," said Software.

Cat-Flap led the way – through the air vent into the cellar, across the ceiling rafters, up through the crack in the floorboards, until they arrived at the sitting-room floor.

The strange snail was nowhere to be seen.

Mr Potter had obviously been in and cleared up his knitting things, and the room was completely deserted. There wasn't even the trace of a trail.

"He's gone!" sobbed Cat-Flap. "Disappeared! Vanished! Vamoosed!"

"I told you he was a bad dream," said User-Friendly, "Now come back and get some sleep."

But Cat-Flap wouldn't give in. "He was here! Right here! Just where I'm crawling now! Look for him! Find him! Get him back!"

Software was disappointed too. It was almost as if what Cat-Flap had seen was the vision he had conjured in his mind.

"You must have imagined it," he said.

Cat-Flap rounded on him in a fury. "It's all your fault Software!" she accused. "He might have heard about the company I keep! Slug company! He might even know my name! And who gave me my name! You did! And what sort of name is Cat-Flap? Common! No wonder he doesn't want to know! I want a new name! An up-to-date name! A name with a bit of class!"

Software was terribly hurt. Cat-Flap had never been unkind to him before; she'd always had a soft spot for him.

"Aw Cat-Flap," Slipper-Sock tried to intervene. "Aren't you taking things a bit too far –?"

"Slipper-Sock's a common name too!" retorted Cat-Flap. "No wonder I got saddled with you!"

It was Slipper-Sock's turn to be hurt. He crawled miserably back to The Hole and shrank into his shell.

It was only the sound of someone coming into the room that persuaded Cat-Flap to return as well. Still she carried on.

"Cat-Flap's a ridiculous name! That was a hi-tech snail and I want a hi-tech name!"

"How about Hi-Fi?" offered Software.

Cat-Flap's face lit up. Her tentacles goggled with delight.

"Hi-Fi!" she cried ecstatically. "Hi-Fi is really high-flown! Hi-Fi is flighty high!"

Happily consoled at last, she settled down to sleep, sighing Hi-Fi to herself.

Not so poor old Software. He kept trying to puzzle things out.

Pythagosaurus Rex? Hi-tech, or prehistoric? Real or imaginary? The mystery got deeper and deeper.

Chapter 4

Tom, Tom, the Knitter's Son

Just as Software had tried to console Cat-Flap, Mrs Potter was trying to console her husband.

"But I *do* like it dear. Really I do. I've always wanted a plant-pot holder. But I haven't got a plant pot any more. Betsy just broke it."

"Then I'll buy you another one," said Mr Potter.

"That's not really the point. You see, your plant-pot holder is woolly, and plant pots – well – they get wet. Plants need water you see. But wool doesn't like water at all. It would soon go rotten and soggy."

"I'll buy you a *dry* plant then," said Mr Potter.

"You mean a cactus? I'm not very fond of cactus –"

"No, I mean a –"

"You *surely* can't mean a plastic plant," said Mrs Potter. "I can't *stand* plastic plants."

There was a pause while Mr Potter sat with hunched-up shoulders, his knitting scrunched up in his fist. He looked a picture of disappointment.

"We could use your holder for something else . . ." suggested Mrs Potter helpfully, "a mug cosy perhaps, or you could try to knit something else. I really think you are very clever to knit something like that first go. Perhaps you could manage some mittens?"

A glint appeared in Mr Potter's eyes. An idea sprouted in his mind; an idea that burst into growth. "Just give me a day or two –" he said, leaping out of his chair, "and I will give you such a plant! A plant unlike any other. The rarest plant in the street. The rarest in the town! The rarest in the whole wide world! A plant that will open your eyes!" and he dashed back in excitement to the sitting room.

There sat Tom, in deep disgust, pretending to look through some books.

Tom had come to the conclusion that he had the most embarrassing family in the world.

His sister was embarrassing because she was better on the skateboard than he was. She even had a better sort of skateboard. Tom's was second-hand, bought from a car boot sale.

His mother was embarrassing because she had a passion for slugs and snails. She even kept a record of their slime trails. She had given a pair of them to the school and prided herself on being an expert.

And now his father had taken up knitting! As if having a father who taught in his school wasn't bad enough, he now had a father who knitted! It was all Mr Scroggles' fault. Mr Scroggles was an old-fashioned headmaster who had got hold of some new-fangled ideas. One of them was knitting for men. It was he who had encouraged Mr Potter.

Max, of course, had found the whole thing hilarious. No matter how hard he tried to keep a straight face, he couldn't help bursting into giggles. Tom was glad to see him go home. So much for their plans for a stall!

Tom had come to a second conclusion, arising out of the first: he was the most unfortunate boy in the world. There were only two choices before him: he must run away from home or do his homework.

He decided on the homework first.

And that was another thing! His homework was incredibly difficult, and his mother had started it all! The snails she had given to the school did slime trails in geometric patterns – triangles, squares, and so on. She had taken Superslug too and explained that she knew him of old; his was the mastermind behind it, he the Pythagoras of slugs!

Of course, none of the children knew who Pythagoras was. Most of them didn't want to – but there were just a few who did.

So guess what? They *all* had to do a project on Pythagoras. They had to find out what geometry was for. Teachers were all the same – Christmas, bonfire night, holidays – teachers *ruined* them by asking you to write about them. And now they couldn't even have a pair of pet snails in the school without having to do a whole project!

"Dad, how do you spell Pythagoras? I can't find it in the dictionary."

"Twenty-one, twenty-two, twenty-three, P, twenty-four, Y, twenty-five, T, twenty-six," went his father, casting on a new row of stitches.

"Dad!" Tom scowled and snarled. "How am I supposed to follow that?"

"Thirty-eight, H, A, G, thirty-nine, O, R, A, forty, S!" went his father.

29

Slamming out of the room in a rage, Tom yelled all the way down the hall, "MUM. WHO WAS PYTHAGORAS?"

Mrs Potter heard him in the kitchen.

Software heard him in The Hole.

It was the question that burned in his brain, echoing all round the cellar, bouncing off the walls of The Hole: *Who was Pythagoras?*

Software couldn't wait to find out.

Chapter 5

Storm in a Jug

"Pythagoras was a philosopher," began Mrs Potter, putting down her potato peeler.

"What's a philosopher?" asked Tom, feeling perplexed now, as well as cross.

"A philosopher is a thinker. We're all thinkers in a way, but philosophers think about life."

"*I* think about life!" declared Tom.

"I'm sure you do," said Mrs Potter, "but philosophers think more deeply. They are especially brilliant and wise."

"That's me all right," thought Software. He had already reached the cellar door, just in time to hear the conversation.

"He lived a very long time ago," went on Mrs Potter.

"*How* long ago?" asked Tom. "I've got to write all this down."

"I'm not quite sure. He was an ancient Greek, which makes him ages ago. He was also a mathematician who said something about right-angled triangles – though they might teach you differently nowadays."

Tom groaned in despair. Pythagoras didn't sound like his sort of person at all.

"Listen," said Mrs Potter, "why don't you go down the road and borrow Mrs Higgins's encyclopaedia? That will tell you what you want to know."

"I'm not *that* interested," Tom grumbled.

"I'll go," volunteered Betsy. "Flying skateboard at your service!"

Betsy was as good as her word. Soon Tom and Mrs Potter were sitting at the table with the encyclopaedia opened between them. Software had stowed himself away inside a jug on a shelf from where he could hear every word.

"Pythagoras was one of the most interesting and puzzling men in history," Mrs Potter read out. "He was born in 580 BC and died in 500 BC."

Tom was puzzled already. Pythagoras must have lived backwards!

"That makes him 1990 plus 580 years ago."

Tom cottoned on and did a quick sum. Two thousand five hundred and seventy years ago! Tom couldn't see what on earth it had to do with him.

"Good gracious!" said Mrs Potter, with sudden, startled interest. "He believed in the transmigration of souls!"

"The whaaaat?" gaped Tom.

"Reincarnation," said Mrs Potter, reading aloud again. "After death, the soul goes to inhabit some other body, sometimes that of an animal."

"Hey!" Betsy chimed in. "Do you think I might come back as a cat?"

"And I'll come back as a dog," growled Tom, gnashing his teeth at Betsy.

"What's more," said Mrs Potter, with mounting amusement and excitement, "Pythagoras wouldn't eat beans! He wouldn't allow his followers to eat them either!"

"What's wrong with beans?" asked Tom.

"He believed that beans have a soul!" exclaimed Mrs Potter.

History suddenly came close to Tom Potter. For the first time in his life, history whispered in his ear. Just think! More than two and a half thousand years ago, human beings stalked the earth as dotty as his own mum and dad! Take this chap Pythagoras – he might have had children of his own.

How embarrassing for them it must have been!

"Here, read it yourself," said Mrs Potter. "It's really interesting. He thought the planets made music as they moved. He wouldn't have meat or woollen clothing. And it explains what he said about triangles."

"But you said he was *brilliant*! And *wise*!" complained Tom.

Mrs Potter returned to her potatoes, musing all the while. It *did* sound very far-fetched. But Mrs Potter thought that life was a bit far-fetched anyway.

"Can you remember what I said about Superslug when he first turned up?" she called out to her children. "Perhaps he is the soul of a genius come back in the body of a snail."

"That was before you found out he was a slug," said Betsy, remembering her mother's disgust.

"It's transmigration all the same," said Mrs Potter, "You never know, there might be something in it."

Talk about a storm in a tea-cup! There was certainly a storm inside the jug – a powerful, Software, brainstorm! The words hurricanoed round his head. He was shell-shocked with the discovery.

Never mind that Pythagoras wasn't a prehistoric snail. Pythagoras was a philosopher! Never mind that Pythagoras hadn't got a shell. Pythagoras had some amazing ideas! Pythagoras was a human being!

As for that stuff about beans – Software had never liked them much anyway. Now he understood why.

But one problem remained: if Pythagoras was a human being and there was no Pythagosauras Rex, what had Cat-Flap seen? Had she imagined it all?

Never mind! It didn't matter for the moment. He had much more important things to think about, much more important things to do!

Chapter 6

Beans Ain't What They Seems

"What's the matter, Software?" asked User-Friendly, peering through one bleary eye. "Don't tell us you're in love too."

"No. I have something important to tell you," said Software with great solemnity. "Are you all listening carefully?"

The snails waited in sullen silence. They were fed up with these interruptions. They'd had hardly a wink of sleep.

"The truth of the matter is –" began Software, "I don't know how you will take this –"

"Get *on* with it," said Whizz-Kid.

"I am not a snail after all," declared Software.

"You *don't* say!" said Whole-Meal with mock surprise.

"You nearly had me fooled," said Fast-Forward.

"You're kidding," said Floppy-Disc.

"I'm not even a slug," said Software, wondering how to break the incredible news. "I AM A HUMAN BEING! MY REAL NAME IS PYTHAGORAS!"

"Is that all?" said the snails with indifference.

"I might have known it," said Slipper-Sock.

"It doesn't surprise me one bit!" said User-Friendly. "Now can we get some sleep?"

Software couldn't believe his ears. Here he was, making the most amazing announcement of all time, and the snails just couldn't care less.

"Don't you understand what I'm saying?" he harangued. "Don't you realise what this means?"

"Sure," said User-Friendly, "but can we talk about it later tonight?"

The snails were about to withdraw into their shells again when Software cleared his throat. He had something else to say.

"Oh, and by the way, you are not to eat any more beans."

"What was that?" said the snails, immediately up in arms, every neck at full stretch.

"No more beans," said Software.

Now beans are to snails what honey is to bears. Broad beans, French beans, dwarf beans, runner beans – snails just love them all. Raw

40

beans, cooked beans, mouldy beans – the
wetter they are, the better. No doubt if they
were given the chance, they would even like
jumping beans and jelly beans.

"That means peas as well," said Software.
"Peas are a sort of bean."

"Have you gone completely off your
trolley?!" said Slipper-Sock, who was looking
forward that very evening to a feast of broad
bean seedlings, just sprouting nicely in the
ground.

"No," answered Software. "It is just my
painful duty to enlighten you. It is sinful to eat
beans. Beans have souls."

"Souls!" spluttered the snails, all at once. "What are they, when they're all there?"

"That's just it," said Software. "They're not there. I mean they are there, but they're invisible. You can't see them."

The snails crinkled up in confusion.

"It's like a spirit," explained Software. "It's alive, but you can't see it."

"Huh! I'd sooner have a shell any day," sniffed Floppy-Disc.

"And when a human dies," Software went on, "this spirit goes into another creature. An animal perhaps, and some vegetables. Definitely into beans."

"Oh! I get you! Human beans!" scoffed Whizz-Kid.

"It's called transmigration," said Software.

"Absolute clap-trap!" snapped Cat-Flap – or rather Hi-Fi, emerging suddenly from her shell in a fine fit of indignation. "It's just because Software doesn't like beans! They give him indigestion. Don't take a blind bit of notice!"

The snails immediately brightened up. This

was more like the Cat-Flap they knew. She carried on, pleased with the impression she was making. It wasn't bad for a grandma snail.

"Tonight we are having a bean feast. We are having a bean bonanza. We are having a GREAT SNAIL BEANO! Slugs will not be invited. Especially not certain slugs – those with crackpot ideas!"

Software was stunned into silence. This *wasn't* the Cat-Flap he knew. Why was she being so spiteful?

"Cat-Flap –" said Slipper-Sock.

"HI-FI!" she reminded him sharply.

"Sorry. Hi-Fi," said Slipper-Sock, before making a bashful announcement. "I've got a new name too. From now on, my name is Fee-Fi –"

Cat-Flap sniffed in contempt.

"– Fo-Fum!" added Slipper-Sock, trying harder than ever to please.

"Fiddle-de-dee!" said Cat-Flap dismissively. She wasn't letting Slipper-Sock steal the scene.

"Never mind about him," she challenged the rest of the snails. "What's *my* name?"

"Idunno," said Idunno.

"You're Hi-Fi. Slipper-Sock is Fee-Fi-Fo-Fum. Software is a human being. And I'm next in line for the throne," said User-Friendly.

Anything for a bit of peace!

Chapter 7

Clicketty-Clack

Tom Potter poked at the beans on his plate with his fork. Baked beans on toast was one of his favourite foods – or at least it had been until now. But now – oh dear!

Baked souls in tomato sauce!

Baked souls with mini sausages!

It didn't bear thinking about!

Tom Potter knew one thing for sure – baked beans would never be the same again. "Crikey!" he thought. "If I carry on thinking like this, I'll end up as dotty as my parents!"

And dotty they certainly were. Over the last few days things had gone from bad to worse. Nothing would be the same again.

In pride of place, on a pedestal, was his dad's knitted plant-pot holder. Inside it was a knitted pot. Inside that was knitted soil. Sprouting from that was a knitted plant, with knitted leaves, knitted stalks, knitted flowers. Red woolly knitted bobble flowers!

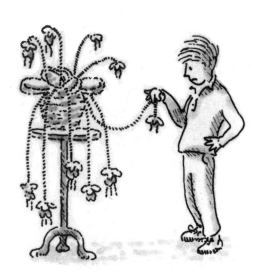

Next, it would be knitted baked beans. Perhaps that's what they were, for they tasted like wool in his mouth.

His Dad was in the sitting room now. Clicketty-clack. Clicketty-clack. Clicketty-clack. The knitting needles sounded in Tom's ears, setting his teeth on edge. He forced himself to swallow the beans, though he wanted to spit them out.

But some things just couldn't be swallowed – like his father knitting at school.

Lately, instead of striding round the classroom as he talked, waving his arms about, scratching his head, feeling in his pockets for his handkerchief, blowing his nose, pelting people with chalk, his dad sat firmly at his desk. Instead of actually teaching, he just set the class some work. Then, while pretending to keep an eye on them, he knitted away under the desk. Max, of course, had spotted the tell-tale strand of wool, the tell-tale movement of the arms, and pointed it out to the other children. The class had dissolved into giggles.

Tom had to do something about it!

He pushed aside the plate of beans and marched purposefully into the sitting room.

"Dad, it's my birthday on Saturday. I want to go to the football match!"

"Knit two together. Pull wool forward. Pick up stitch below," went Mr Potter.

"Dad. Will you help me make a kite?"

Mr Potter brightened at this and put down his knitting for a second. "Make you a kite! Of course I will. Just let me finish this and I'll *knit* you a kite!"

"Dad! Why don't you watch the boxing on the telly? Why don't you go to the pub and have a beer? Why don't you fix the rust marks on the car?"

"Five rows in rib. Five rows in stocking stitch. Alternate rows in garter," said his father, jotting down the pattern as he went.

"DAD! WHY DON'T YOU DO THE SORT OF THINGS DADS ARE SUPPOSED TO DO?" bawled Tom at the top of his voice.

"Whatever are you shouting for Tom?" asked his mother, rushing in from the garden.

"Look at him! Just look at him!" raged Tom. "That man is my father. What sort of example is *that* to a growing boy? How can I look up to *him*?"

"Shhhhh!" went Mrs Potter, dragging Tom out of the room. "You mustn't say things like that. You'll hurt your father's feelings. There's no reason why a man shouldn't knit. It's a very soothing thing to do – and much healthier than smoking cigarettes. And he's not the only one. Why – I was reading the other day about a bishop who knits cardigans. He even knitted himself a mitre! And there's this chap called Kaffe Fasset who knits beautiful, wonderful –"

"I don't care about Faffy Kasset!" yelled Tom. "I want a proper dad! I want a dad who shows me how to mend a puncture. I want a dad who makes model aeroplanes. I want a dad with smelly socks who smokes a pipe! What's more, it's my birthday on Saturday and I want a dad who takes notice of me!"

"So it is," said Mrs Potter. "Come to think of it, it's also our wedding anniversary. We must think of something special to do."

Clicketty-clack, clicketty-clack went the needles. Mr Potter was concentrating hard, obviously so deeply inspired that he was oblivious to the row outside the door.

Chapter 8

The Mystery Unravels

Not content with her new name – or title – as she preferred to call it, Hi-Fi was busy tidying up The Hole.

"Look at those soggy leaves! Clear away that crisp packet! Get rid of those cobwebs!" she ordered, bossing the others about.

Slipper-Sock was all forlorn. "But Cat-Flap – " he kept saying dolefully.

"HI-FI!" she insisted. "And stop that drivelling and drooling. Pull yourself together!"

Soon The Hole was so spick and span the snails felt like moving out.

But Hi-Fi didn't care. All she could think

about was the lime-green snail in the sitting room. He had to be lured out of hiding. He needed to be enticed. But how, into a place so damp, so dusty, so dirty? She knew there wasn't a chance. A good sprucing up was a must.

"Come on!" she cajoled. "Use a bit of elbow grease! Let's see some more spit and polish!"

"I don't know about that," grumbled Whizz-Kid. "I've used up most of next week's slime."

"Can't you do something about her?" User-Friendly kept asking Software.

As it happened, there was no need. Fate stepped in and took a hand. It was Whizz-Kid who broke the news, early one evening when the snails were just awake and Software wasn't even around.

"I've seen him!" he spluttered in excitement.

"He's there! I saw his shadow against the wall!"

"Who? What? Where?" asked the snails.

"Hi-Fi's hi-tech snail! Up in the sitting room. He's enormous! Gigantic! Terrifying! And his tail really *is* two-pronged! And he makes the most peculiar noises. Listen! Just listen and you'll hear it!"

The snails listened with straining ears, catching the faintest sound. Clicketty-clack, clicketty-clack, clicketty-clack.

All of a flutter with excitement, Hi-Fi led the way, while the snails followed cautiously behind.

They peeped through the crack in the floorboards.

Sure enough! Cast on the wall was a shadow, a sinister silhouette. It looked like a giant snail, with the spikiest tentacles and tail.

"You're chief, User-Friendly. You should go first," said Hi-Fi, suddenly overcome with shyness.

But it was Slipper-Sock who went charging forward. Slipper-Sock was ready to do battle, ready to defend what was his own.

The snails gathered under the sofa, from where they watched his fearless approach. The strange snail made no move at all.

They saw Slipper-Sock's expression change, from ferocity, to utter surprise. They saw him sniff hard in bewilderment. Then they saw him smile.

And no wonder! For Hi-Fi's hi-tech snail was nothing but a ball of wool, stuck with two steel needles, with a lime-green strand trailing behind.

A woolly, not a slimy strand, leading from Mr Potter's knitting bag.

Mr Potter sat on the sofa, his arms working furiously away, his desk lamp shining behind him.

User-Friendly spoke gently to Cat-Flap. "Hi-Fi. You must be getting a little short-sighted. That isn't a snail at all. That is a ball of wool. Those tentacles are steel needles with knobs. Its tail is the pointed ends."

"No! Never!" gasped Hi-Fi. "You're just trying to pull the wool over my eyes. You're just a spoil-sport and a kill-joy. You don't want me to have any fun!"

But as if further proof were needed, Mr Potter suddenly seized her beloved and pulled out his tentacles and tail. Even worse was to follow. To the clicketty-clack of steel needles, her beloved began slowly to unwind.

Soon there was nothing left.

Cat-Flap burst into tears. This time she couldn't even blame Software.

"Suppertime!" called Mrs Potter from the kitchen.

Mr Potter heard her, and put down his knitting for a while.

The snails also took the hint, and set off via The Hole for the garden, with Hi-Fi in a very sniffy huff.

Software wasn't interested in supper. From a leaf on the knitted plant, he was trying to puzzle things out.

If he had indeed the soul of a human being, why had he come back as a slug? And which human beings had he been? Apart from Pythagoras, that is. He might have been others in between.

Had he even been – a bean? A has-bean, you might say. What would he come back as next?

He simply had to find out.

There was one way he could try. Since he couldn't convince the snails that he had once been a human being, he must try to convince the humans.

But how?

By acting like one himself!

He saw his opportunity now. The family was sitting down to eat and there was human-looking food on the table, set out on human-looking dishes.

Only once before had Software dared openly to approach the humans. That had been a long time ago, to warn Mrs Potter of danger. The result had been disastrous. She had promptly hoovered him up!

But Betsy and Tom had come to the rescue. His hopes were on Betsy now.

Slowly, with all the grace and courage he could muster, Software made his way to the table top.

It was Tom who spotted him first.

But there came no mighty SPLATTTT! Instead, the whole family froze.

Slowly and deliberately, trying to look as human as possible, Software crawled towards Betsy's plate.

Betsy turned a pale shade of green.

"Get rid of it!" hissed Mr Potter.

"But it might be Superslug," said his wife. "We must wait to see what he does. He might be trying to tell us something."

Software crawled on to Betsy's plate.

He crept up to her slice of bread.

He daintily took a bite.

But he was no frog from a fairy-tale. Betsy didn't give him a kiss, and he didn't turn into a prince. Instead the door suddenly burst open.

"Hope you don't mind my barging in," said Mrs Higgins breezily. "I wondered if you'd finished with my encyclopaedia? And can I borrow your garden roller?"

A hand clapped down over Software. Luckily, a cup-shaped hand. With truly undignified haste, he was bundled outside into the yard.

Chapter 9

Knit-Knacks

"Good gracious! What's this?!" exclaimed Mrs Potter on the morning of her wedding anniversary. She had only just opened her eyes.

On the bed before her Mr Potter had placed a tray. On the tray was a cup of tea, a flower in a vase, and a boiled egg in an egg-cup with soldiers.

Everything but the tray was knitted!

"Well! My word!" gasped Mrs Potter. "I don't know *what* to say. You've certainly picked up this knitting business quickly. Why, I couldn't even knit a dishcloth if I tried!"

Then Mr Potter gave her a real cup of tea, and a real boiled egg with soldiers.

"This is called having your breakfast and eating it," said Mrs Potter cheerily, admiring her knitted boiled egg.

Then Betsy gave her a present.

It was a tin-toy clockwork snail with a black and yellow striped shell, and springy, red-bobble tentacles. Mrs Potter wound him up and he crawled across the breakfast tray with a life-like sway from side to side.

Then Tom gave her a present.

It was a pottery snail money box with a slot in the top of its shell and there were two baby china snails to go with it.

"I'll soon have quite a collection," said Mrs Potter, thinking of the brass snail she had given herself.

Tom Potter kept quiet all the while. He had already opened two of his birthday presents – a new computer game and a kit-bag. His main present was yet to come. Tom had spotted the parcel, and it made him feel very excited. It was a skateboard-shaped parcel. A bigger-and-better-than-Betsy's-skateboard-shaped parcel. Tom was looking forward to opening it – but didn't mind postponing the pleasure.

"I've got a special present for you too," said Mr Potter to his wife, "I'll give it to you later. I've got to add the finishing touch."

Downstairs in the sitting room Software Superslug was gazing at this self-same special present, minus its finishing touch. He was agog with wonder and amazement.

Before him, on the pouffe, was a lime-green knitted slug.

A slug, and not a snail.

Pythagosaurus Rex, no doubt! So he *did* exist after all.

Things suddenly came right for Software: he could forget about being a snail; he needn't bother about being a human being. With a monument like this to do him honour, it was perfectly all right to be a slug. His dignity was more than restored!

He was so excited that he went racing back to The Hole to fetch the snails. They simply *had* to see this. *This* would show Hi-Fi.

"Hi-Fi! User-Friendly! Floppy-Disc! Whizz-Kid! Idunno! Fast-Forward! Whole-Meal! Slipper-Sock! Wake up! Come and see! Come and see!"

But snails that are snoozing in the daytime are notoriously hard to wake up – especially in a manner such as this. And Software wasn't popular at the moment. He kept nagging them not to eat beans.

"Whassermarrer? Whassermarrer?" burbled User-Friendly, and when Software gabbled on about something knitted in the sitting room, all he could do was groan. "Oh no! Not another one! We've already been through all that!"

So Software was forced to bribe them. It was only when he had told the snails where the new bean sowings were, that the snails allowed themselves to be hustled together and driven up to the sitting room.

And then, oh dear, what a shock!

To Pythagosaurus Rex, the giant lime-green slug, Mr Potter had added the finishing touch.

A giant knitted shell! In glorious speckledy browns.

The slug had become a snail!

Next to it was a brass snail, and a clockwork snail, and a pottery snail, and two baby china snails. There was even a snail-shaped card.

Software shrivelled up with disappointment.

Not so Hi-Fi. Hi-Fi was blinking with delight. She was in love all over again!

"He's wonderful! He's gorgeous! He's *cuddly*!" she cried. "He's simply *got* to be mine!"

Chapter 10

Curiouser and Curiouser

In the living room at that moment, Tom Potter was trying to hold back the tears as he looked at his birthday present.

Oh yes – it was a skateboard all right, but not bigger and better than Betsy's. Tom's skateboard was knitted!

"Oh Dad!" Tom gulped in dismay.

His Dad mistook the gulp. He thought it showed delighted surprise. He was so wrapped up in his knitting that he didn't see how anyone could fail to be pleased.

"I bet you haven't seen a skateboard like *that* before, have you Tom?" said Mr Potter.

"No Dad. I haven't –" said Tom, but before

he could say any more Mrs Potter nudged him with her elbow and gave him a meaningful look.

Tom thought he understood. The knitted skateboard was only a joke, like the knitted boiled egg and toast fingers. He had only to wait a while before his father would produce one bigger-and-better-than-Betsy's.

But no. His father disappeared into the sitting room and the clicketty-clack began again.

Tom looked imploringly at his mother.

"I'm sorry Tom," she said. "I didn't know what he was up to. He was just so secretive about it."

Tom went after his dad, determined to have things out. His mother pulled him back. "No Tom," she warned. "You mustn't say a word! Grown-ups go through phases just the same as children. Your father is going through a phase. He's been under a lot of strain. Don't worry, it'll pass."

"But I want a skateboard I can *skate* on," protested Tom. "That looks like a scarf on wheels."

"You can borrow my skateboard for the day," offered Betsy.

"That's not the *same!*"

There was a trundling sound up the drive.

It was Mrs Higgins, returning the roller.

"Hallo everyone," she called, walking in as she usually did. Her eyes lit upon the skateboard.

"Good heavens! What's this?" she enthused.

70

"I've never seen anything like this!"

"It's a skateboard. Tom's birthday present from his father," said Mrs Potter.

"But *where* did he get it?"

"He knitted it."

"But *how?*" said Mrs Higgins, examining the skateboard more closely. "Oh I see, it's got a cardboard frame. And the wheels! They look so realistic! It's so *witty!* So *ingenious!* Tom, what a lucky boy you are!"

Tom just shrugged and scowled.

"Do you think I could borrow it?" begged Mrs Higgins. "Of course, only for a while, when you've enjoyed it to the full. But my brother has a sports shop you see, over in Leamington Spa. If he put this in his window, what a show-stopper it would be!"

"Uh. Sure. Yeah," mumbled Tom.

"And what's *this*?" exclaimed Mrs Higgins, spotting the breakfast tray. "A knitted boiled egg! A knitted cup of tea! Knitted toast fingers! And *look* at that knitted plant! Why, this gets curiouser and curiouser! Your husband is an *artist*, Mrs Potter. He has a truly original *talent*!

Look, you just tell him to knit a few more things like this and I'll get my friend Mr Mustique to arrange an exhibition. He runs the Old Hat gallery in town. He'd absolutely *adore* these things!"

"There's something else in the sitting room," said Mrs Potter, taking Mrs Higgins to see the knitted snail.

Mr Potter ignored them, oblivious to all but his knitting.

Oblivious, as well, to the goings-on on the window seat.

Snuggled up to the knitted snail was Hi-Fi; she *refused* to be parted from it. Nose-to-nose with the brass snail was Whizz-Kid; he just *couldn't* tear himself away. Between the two baby china snails was Whole-Meal; she'd fallen for them on sight. On the money box snail was Slipper-Sock, *fascinated* by the slot. Going from one to the other, as if he didn't know which he liked best, was a very muddled Idunno.

Software was nowhere to be seen.

"Good gracious!" said Mrs Potter. "It looks as though we've got quite a gathering!"

"Oh!" gasped Mrs Higgins, with a shuddering, shivery smile. "Just look at that knitted snail! I can see why it's caused such a stir. At the Old Hat it will be a sensation! Do you mind if I take it now?"

At this, the snails quietly scarpered. All except Hi-Fi that is. Unknown to Mrs Higgins, Hi-Fi hung on tight.

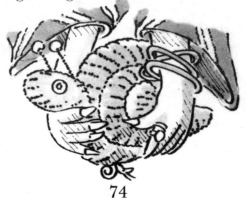

Chapter 11

Like Father, Like Son

The following week was half-term. Tom was busy in secret. Since Max and he had fallen out, he worked by himself on his stall for the school fête.

An enormous cardboard carton outside a freezer shop had given him a new idea: a teacher-nut shy. He'd make cardboard cut-outs of the teachers and for 5p a go the children could say all the things they wanted to say to them but daren't. Then they could pelt them with paint blobs. He'd started with a model of his dad.

Mr Potter was busy too – knitting for his exhibition.

From the ends of his knitting needles, things wondrous and strange took shape. He knitted a plate of fish and chips, complete with mushy peas. He knitted an ultra-modern telephone. He knitted a birthday cake with candles and he knitted a prize-size leek.

It was as if the wool unwound, not from the basket on the floor, but from the very inside of himself, rather like the trail of a snail. And it was as if he didn't just knit with his hands, but with his heart and mind and soul, not to mention an odd sense of humour.

Mrs Higgins had talked to Mr Mustique and the exhibition was all arranged. To Mr Potter it was the opportunity of a life-time – his chance of escape from the classroom. His true vocation was discovered. He knitted all day long.

But occasionally, he did have to stop. Since not one member of the family was willing to feed him while he knitted, he had to stop for meals. And since not one member of the family could go to the lavatory for him, he had to go for himself.

On one of his trips to the bathroom he heard a strangled, choking voice, coming from behind Tom's door. At first, he thought Tom was playing one of his Tin-Tin tapes. But when he listened more carefully, he realised it was Tom's own voice, and when he put his ear to the door, he could hear what Tom was saying.

"You! Oh you! You're the worst dad a boy ever had! A cissy! A soppy! A nit-wit!"

Stab! Snip! Scrunch!

"Don't you ever think about me? You know

I wanted to go to the motor show and all you do is sit and knit! You know what they used to call you at school? They called you Dotty Potter! You know what they call you now? Twitty the nutty nit! Knitty the twitty nut! Do you know what that's like for me? Do you? Do you *even care*?! You're embarrassing! You're excruciating! You're a – a –"

Crunch! Snip! Munch!

For the first time in several days, Mr Potter forgot all about knitting.

Whoever was Tom talking to?

Whatever was he doing?

Had the poor boy gone off his head?

As quietly as he could, so as not to startle his son, Mr Potter opened the door.

Tom stood there with his back turned. He was obviously in a mad fit of rage.

Then Mr Potter saw what he talked to.

It was an enormous cardboard carton with a cartoon figure on the side. Tom was angrily cutting it out.

"What's that Tom?" Mr Potter gently enquired.

Tom gave a guilty start.

"A secret," he said, wondering how much his dad had overheard and trying to hide what he was doing.

But Mr Potter had seen already. "What an interesting idea," he said thoughtfully. "Man breaking out of his box."

Tom looked at his father in bewilderment.

"Don't you see Tom?" said Mr Potter. "That's just what I'm doing with my knitting – breaking out of my box – doing something men aren't supposed to do. And that figure is really good. It looks just like me."

This was too much for Tom. "Well I wish you'd get back into your box and stay there – *with the lid on!*" he blurted out.

"Oh dear," said Mr Potter. "You *are* upset. I think you'd better tell me all about it."

And Tom did. Mr Potter listened calmly. Although his head was mostly full of knitting, he could dimly remember what he had been like as a boy – and yes – it had to be admitted; he would not have liked a father who knitted.

Even more important, his worst fears had proved groundless. Tom hadn't been talking to himself.

They were unravelling all this between them when Mrs Potter called up the stairs.

"Arnold! Tom! Mrs Higgins to see you!"

"Look Tom. Does this have to stay a secret? It might be just the thing we need to advertise my exhibition."

"No . . . well . . . all right."

"You go," said Mr Potter. "I'll be down in a minute."

"Tom," said Mrs Higgins, "I don't know quite how to ask you – but – well – my brother is so thrilled with the knitted skateboard – sales are simply soaring – he wondered if you might loan it to him for a bit longer – until your father has time to knit another one? In return, you can go to the shop and choose any skateboard you like."

"To keep?" asked Tom.

"To keep," said Mrs Higgins.

No sooner was this agreed than the strangest figure came shuffling down the stairs: a cartoon of Mr Potter, half cut out of a cardboard carton!

Mrs Higgins gaped.

"How about this?" said a muffled voice from behind the box.

"What an amazing contraption!" said Mrs Higgins.

"That's what I thought," said Mr Potter poking his head out from the side. "It's me, you see. 'Man breaking out of his box'. Get it? It's Tom's idea."

"Brrrilliant!" gasped Mrs Higgins. "And the likeness is extraordinary. Just put some knitting in its hands and it's the perfect thing for publicity."

"What do you say Tom?" asked Mr Potter.

Tom shrugged, smiled and sighed. Would he ever understand grown-ups?

"I hoped you'd agree," said Mr Potter. "Like father, like son, as they say."

Chapter 12

At the Old Hat

The day came for the exhibition to open. There was to be a preview with a glass of wine for specially invited guests and the Potter family nervously awaited their arrival.

"Do you think anyone will come?" Betsy whispered to Tom.

"I hope not," answered Tom, though he didn't really mean it. A whole day spent on his spiffing new skateboard had made him realise that a boy must stand by his father, no matter how odd his ways. And Max had come to help serve the wine.

Two old ladies wandered in. To the "Man Breaking Out of His Box", one offered 5p from her purse.

"It must be free," said her friend, when the figure made no move to take it.

They stood and gazed around for a while, their eyes travelling from the plate of knitted fish and chips to the knitted knicker-bocker glory, from the knitted flowering plant to the knitted pair of knobbly knees.

"Oh dear," said one of them faintly, "I think I've come over all funny."

Then her friend saw Mrs Potter. "We were hoping to find a nice pair of bed-socks," she said, "or perhaps a tea-cosy."

Mr Mustique stepped in. "This is an *art* exhibition, not a knitting bazaar! But welcome, welcome, dear ladies. Have a glass of wine."

Gradually the gallery filled up.

Wine flowed, cheeks flushed, tongues wagged, praise gushed, but no red stickers appeared to show that a thing had been sold.

Tom began to feel sorry for his dad. "Don't worry," he said. "Things will soon pick up."

Suddenly, from the stand by the knitted snail there came a terrific screech.

"OOOOAAAGH! Look at that! There's a creeeechure crawling up the wall!"

It was Miss Dangle from Dingle Dell Arts.

Other voices joined in. "Ooooogh. Ugh. Ow. Get rid of it. It's slimy."

"Revolting!"

"Spoiling your nice clean wall!"

The "creechure" in question was Hi-Fi, trying to make her escape. She'd been clinging all the while to her beloved cuddly snail, but realised her love was not returned. What's more, the crowding voices alarmed her.

Mr Mustique rushed over with a dust-pan and brush and would have swept Hi-Fi into the bin, when Mrs Potter came to the rescue.

"No! Don't! That's a rare and endangered species!"

"It looks like a common garden snail to me," said Miss Dangle, with obvious distaste.

"Oh no," said Mrs Potter, gently picking Hi-Fi up. "This is a tawny-mottled mollusc. A genuine gastropod. It must be returned to its natural habitat."

"Hold it!" said a photographer. "I'm from the local press."

And so, with the knitted snail and a real snail, Mrs Potter had her photograph taken. Then, Tom and his father had their picture taken with "Man Breaking Out of His Box".

Even so, they were disappointed. Apart from the knitted snail, which both of the two old ladies wanted to buy after two glasses of wine, not a single thing had been sold.

"Name your price!" said one old lady to Mrs Potter.

"Double it!" said the other.

But Mrs Potter wouldn't part with the knitted snail. It was her special anniversary present after all. Home it went with Hi-Fi, the one let loose in the garden, the other put back on the pouffe.

Mr Potter gave a gloomy sigh. "Oh well, we must take these things in our stride."

Chapter 13

Fame at Last

Early the following evening, Tom came rushing in from the hall with the Evening Gazette in his hands.

"Hey Dad! We're in the paper! And Mum too!"

Sure enough, on the "What's New" pages was a photograph of Mrs Potter with a real snail and a knitted snail, and Mr Potter and Tom with the "Box".

"And that's my hand!" said Betsy, pointing to a corner of the picture.

Mr Potter looked at the headline.

"Come on, read it out'" said Mrs Potter eagerly. Mr Potter began:

NEW VIEWS FROM A NOVELTY KNITTER
or
MAN BREAKING OUT OF HIS BOX

So you think that knitting is for women? Think again! Here is a man who has broken the mould.

In the natty novelty knitting designs of Mr Arnold Potter everything breaks the mould. Nothing is what you expect. Fish and chips – in garter stitch! Birthday cake – in Fair Isle! Knobbly knees – in stocking stitch! Boiled egg – in four ply. Snail – in rib! You name it – he knits it!

By changing the way you see things, he changes the way you think. He makes you ask yourself the question: *why are things the way they are?* Or to take the question one step further – *are they the way they are? Are they knitted or knot?*

It takes only a small leap of the imagination to see the Almighty as The Great Knitter, knitting an expanding Universe.

And where does Mankind fit into all this? ·Mankind is a *dropped stitch –?*

"– which womankind is forever trying to pick up!" quipped Mrs Potter.

"Blimey!" said Tom. "Who wrote that?"

"What does it mean?" asked Betsy.

"It means it's a rave review!" said a delighted Mrs Potter, giving her husband a hug. "Congratulations!"

The telephone started to ring. It was Mr Mustique from the Old Hat gallery. He had news for Mr Potter. Since the review had appeared *his* telephone hadn't stopped ringing. Everything, yes everything, had been sold! And there were orders for even more!

"Well well well . . ." said Mr Potter, beaming all over his face. "Well well well well well . . ."

Even Tom was impressed.

"Well well well," said User-Friendly to Hi-Fi. "Look who's returned to the fold."

Hi-Fi told them all about it.

"It was terrible!" she said with a shudder. "I was led completely astray! This gallery place! All so clean and clinical! Not a soggy leaf or a cobweb in sight! Nothing to comfort poor snails! And you should have heard those people! All so hoity-toity! All so la-di-dah! All so − so −"

"High falutin'?" put in Slipper-Sock.

"That's it! High falutin'! Stuck up! Do you know what they said about me? They all said 'OOOOOAAAGH!' Now I know how Software must feel! But that nice Mrs Potter stuck up for me! I am not Hi-Fi any more! She had some other names for me! Like Tawny-Mottled Mollusc! Like Rare and Endangered Species! I haven't a clue what they mean. So . . . why don't we settle for Cat-Flap?"

"Oh Cat-Flap," sighed Slipper-Sock, giving her a big fat kiss.

"Software will tell you what they mean," said User-Friendly. "They sound like something important."

"But where *is* Software?" asked Cat-Flap. "We must try to make up to him. We must show him some sympathy."

"Idunno," said Idunno.

"We thought he was with you," said Floppy-Disc.

The awful truth dawned on the snails. Software had been missing for nights!

What if he never came back?

Life without Software was unthinkable! Life without Software was unimaginable! Life without Software would be terrible – not to mention a bit short on beans.

"We must send out a search party," said User-Friendly, "or we're in for some very hard times."

Chapter 14

Slugs, Bugs and Millepedes

The snails waited for night to fall and then set out on their search.

They roamed all over the garden, looking under every stone, but Software wasn't there.

They scoured every inch of the cellar, every crack in every beam, but Software was nowhere to be seen.

They even searched the potting shed and at one point Cat-Flap thought she had found him. But it was only a picture on a packet with "SLUG DEATH" written underneath.

Their last hope was the sitting room.

"How do we even know what we're looking for?" asked Whizz-Kid. "You never know – he might have done that transmigration thing – died and come back as something else."

"He might even be a chair!" said Whole-Meal.

"A fly!" said Slipper-Sock.

"A lump of coal!" said Floppy-Disc, searching the coal scuttle.

"A bean!" gulped Slipper-Sock, thinking guiltily of the bean he'd just eaten.

"Software! Software! Where are you?" they called, frantically circling the pouffe.

Suddenly, there was a feeble answer. "I'm here. Here! In here!"

With tentacles standing to attention, the snails looked anxiously round. The voice came from the knitted snail.

"Whizz-Kid, you were right! He's come back as a knitted snail!"

"He *can't* have!" protested Cat-Flap.

"No, no, no," gasped the voice. "I'm trapped inside this woolly shell. I'm starving. I'm suffocating. I'm dying . . ."

Poor old Software Superslug!

From the moment he had set eyes on Pythagosaurus Rex, he had been in a terrible state.

His first feeling was deep disappointment. Somehow, the knitted slug was a symbol – something that stood for all slugs, giving them a new kind of status. Software had felt so proud, the equal of any snail.

Then came the finishing touch. Mr Potter had added the shell. The slug had become a snail – and all Software's longings came back. A shared shell, he decided, was better than no shell at all. Even a knitted shared shell.

Through a gap in the stitches that fixed the shell on to the snail Software had found a way in. Then he had started to crawl – along the long coiled tube Mr Potter had knitted, wound round in the shape of a shell.

Round, round, round, Software had crawled, along the winding woolly way. The fit got tighter and tighter. There was less and less air to breathe. Then, when he had got to the end, to the very small middle of the shell, he couldn't turn round to come back. He had tried crawling backwards for a while, but had given up in despair.

He was desperately, horribly, stuck.

What could he do but think? He had stayed there, thinking for hours.

What a failure he felt!

He had failed to convince the snails he was a snail without a shell, and failed to convince the humans that he was really one of them.

So what was he, when all was said and done? Did he have a human soul? If so, why had he returned as a slug?

"Perhaps," he said to himself, "I had to discover that every creature counts – even the most humble and despised, even the most disgusting. For nothing is more so than a slug. That's it," he had decided. "I Software Superslug, unlovely, unlovable and unloved, count for something!

"All the slugs, bugs and millepedes! They too, count for something.

"Everything that lives counts for something!"

But so starved was he inside the shell, of air, of food, of space, that he now counted for very nearly nothing. When the snails, with a tremendous chomping of jaws, chewed their way through the shell, it was a faint and enfeebled slug that emerged, a shadow of his former self.

"I'll be all right," he gasped. "Just give me some time on my own. Just give me some time to recover."

Watched sadly by the snails, he crawled towards his favourite armchair, till he was lost on its underside.

There he decided to stay.

Chapter 15

Not the End

There is something strange about elephants; they know when they are going to die.

Then they make their secret way through the jungle, to the ancient, elephant graveyard. They lie down among the bones and ivory tusks. In peace they breathe their last.

So it was with Software, except that there was no slug graveyard, only his favourite armchair.

Some days later, Mrs Potter was looking critically at this very same armchair. The loose cover was rather grubby. Now that her husband was a celebrity, there was a constant stream of visitors to the house – photographers, gallery owners, and the like. The loose cover could do with a wash.

She unzipped the cover at the side and was pulling it up and off, when she saw something really strange on the calico back of the chair.

In wobbly, joined up writing, rather dried and brown, Mrs Potter read:

not the end

At the end of the trail was a small brown creature. Mrs Potter knew who he was. She had seen that writing once before. It had to be Superslug. No longer sleek and shiny, Software was

> quite
>
> > quite
> >
> > > dead!

Mrs Potter tried to hold back the tears. After all, he was only a slug. She couldn't cry over a slug.

Soon she was weeping profusely.

Betsy came into the room. She had come to show her mother her knitting. Now that Mr Potter was famous, novelty knitting had really caught on. Even Max was knitting something, like most of the children at school. Only Tom still refused.

Betsy saw what there was to see.

"Oh Mum," she said. "You can't be upset about that! After all, he was only a slug!"

Soon Betsy was weeping as well.

Tom came down to see what the matter was. "This is ridiculous!" he said, "all over one small slug!"

The tears tumbled down, just the same.

Mr Potter came into the room. "I can't have this," he said, "not over an insignificant little slug. There are plenty more where he came from."

"But we've got used to having him around," wailed Betsy. "He's *special*!"

"We've got to *know* him," sobbed Tom.

Mr Potter joined in. The family had a good long cry.

Then they went into mourning.

They buried Software with ceremony. Betsy placed him on a lettuce leaf in a matchbox with a bit of cucumber and tomato. Tom inscribed a slate for a headstone, scratching in the letters with a nail, ghostly white on grey. Betsy made a glazed pottery slug, a monument to a very old friend. They chose a spot by the strawberry bed.

That night, when the snails were out in the garden, Cat-Flap suddenly called. "Hey! It's Software! It's Software! I've found him!"

All the snails came over to look.

Fast-Forward crept up close. This Software was very still. He was also very hard. "Software hasn't *got* a shell," said Fast-Forward. "Software *is* a shell."

"No, no," said User-Friendly, wisely shaking his head. "Look, there's some squiggles on that headstone:

HERE LIES SUPERSLUG. GENIUS.
R.I.P."

he just managed to read out.

"They didn't know he was called Software," gulped Whole-Meal.

"It was nice of them to make him a statue," sobbed Floppy-Disc. "At least they cared. Humans aren't altogether awful."

"Yes they are!" said Whizz-Kid. "I don't *like* sad endings! Sad endings shouldn't be allowed!"

"It isn't really sad," said User-Friendly. "It isn't even the end. We've still got to say our farewells."

Then the snails had a great snail funeral, with a great snail funeral feast to follow.

"Do you think he *will* come back as something else?" asked Slipper-Sock, tucking into a tulip shoot.

"Course he will," said Cat-Flap, nibbling a sweet pea seedling. "Can you imagine a character like Software resting in peace for long? Oh no! Not him! He'll get an idea into his head about what he wants to be next, then – hey presto! – he'll be back!"

"But what as?" asked several snails at once.

"Idunno," said Idunno. "Idunno. Idunno. Idunno."

"But I do," said a voice from behind them; a friendly, familiar voice,

Slowly the snails looked round. The strangest sight met their eyes – a sight that filled them with amazement.

"What happened?" they all gasped at once.

"You'll never guess –" began the voice.

But the rest is another story.